Business Plan Example - An Internet Company

By
Kris Solie-Johnson

Published by
American Institute of Small Business
7515 Wayzata Blvd, Suite 129
Minneapolis, MN 55426
952-545-7001
www.aisb.biz
info@aisb.biz

TABLE OF CONTENTS

INTRODUCTION

Going into business, either independently or with others, is a dream that most Americans would like to fulfill during their lifetime. Each year more than 1 million new businesses start up, while more than three to four times that number never leave the planning or thinking stage.

It has often been said that SMALL BUSINESSES come and go just like NIGHT and DAY. How often have you driven by a shopping center one week and observed a sign announcing a "GRAND OPENING"; then, within one year, driven by the same location, this time seeing a new sign saying: "GOING OUT OF BUSINESS SALE"?

How often do we hear stories about people and companies having a close or enter bankruptcy? And why is it that we keep hearing statistics that say: 9 out of 10 new businesses fail or close within the first two years of operations?

The answer can be found in any number of reasons. These reasons include:

- LOW SALES VOLUME
- INSUFFICIENT CAPITAL
- WRONG LOCATION
- INCORRECT MERCHANDISE
- COMPETITION IS TOO STRONG
- INEFFECTIVE ADVERTISING
- CHANGING MARKET CONDITIONS
- POOR MANAGEMENT
- LACK OF KNOW HOW

One could list a dozen more reasons why businesses fail. Regardless of the reason, the one way of **INSURING** a much higher degree of success when starting or opening a new business, expanding and diversifying an existing business or, even continuing with a current ongoing successful business is to have a **BUSINESS PLAN**.

**A Business Plan is necessary for any business,
even an Internet Business.**

WHY WRITE A BUSINESS PLAN?

There are many reasons why a business plan should be prepared. Regardless of the specific reason, the underlying goal of preparing a business plan is to insure the success of the business. In the end, a good business plan will give you a "GO" or "NO GO" answer for your business before you have invested all your time and money. Here are the other reasons why a business plan should be prepared:

1. To provide you with the ROAD MAP that you need in order to run your business. It allows you to make detours, change directions, and alter the pace that you set in starting and running the business.

2. To assist you in financing. Whether one is starting up a small business or buying a business, banks and financial institutions want to see that you know where you are, where you are going, and how you are going to get there.

3. To tell you how much money you need, when you will need it, and how you are going to get it and pay it back. In other words, how you will do your financing?

4. To help you clearly think through what type of business you are starting, and allows you to consider every aspect of that business.

5. To raise questions in a systematic way that you need to have the answered in order to succeed in your business.

6. To establish a system of checks and balances for your business so that you avoid mistakes.

7. To set up bench marks to keep your business under control.

8. To help you develop the COMPETITIVE SPIRIT to make you keenly prepared and ready to operate.

9. To make you think through the entire business process so that you do not open the business blindly or lack vital information in opening and maintaining your business.

10. To force you to analyze the competition.

AISB Quickie Business Plan

Page 1   **Introduction**

Company Name: _____

Date: _____

Your Name: _____

Your Idea/Concept: _____

Page 2   **Evaluating Ideas and Concepts**

Does the Test Market like our idea?_____

What did they like about it? _____

How many said they will buy it? _____

What price were they willing to pay?_____

Why would they buy ours vs. competition?_____

What need are we filling? _____

Page 3   **Researching Your Idea**

Industry opportunities/challenges:_____

Market size: _____

Competition strengths:_____

Site Location: _____

Business Formation: _____

Page 4   **Preliminary Planning**

Financial Plan

Start Up Costs: _____

Sales: Yr 1 _____ Yr 2 _____

Expenses: Yr 1 _____ Yr 2 _____

Profits: Yr 1 _____ Yr 2 _____

Marketing Plan

Product: _____

Price: _____

Promotion: _____

_____

Place: _____

Selling Plan: _____

Operation Plan

Units built: _____

Total Cost: _____

Unit Cost: _____

Page 5   **Getting Money**

Amount Needed: _____

Borrowed $: _____

Cash on Hand: _____

Cash for Equity of Company: _____ Equity given up: _____%

Page 6   **Setting Up The Business**

People Needed: _____

Duties: _____

Technology Needed: _____

Advisors: _____   _____

_____   _____

Suppliers: _____   _____

_____   _____

BUSINESS PLAN OUTLINE

I. Cover Sheet and Table of Contents

II. Executive Summary

    A. Mission Statement

    B. Description of the Business

        1. Overall purpose of the business

        2. Specific purpose of the business

    C. Marketing Strategy

    D. Production Process

    E. Management Team

    F. Objectives of the Team

    G. Financial Considerations

        1. Income Statements (3 years)

        2. Balance Sheet Projections (3 years)

        3. Cash flow Projections (1 year)

III. Company Information

    A. Location(s)

        1. Location costs

        2. Location benefits

    B. Suppliers

IV. Industry, Market and Competition

    A. What is the Industry – Definition

        1. Background of industry

2. Trade Associations

3. Publications

4. Industry trends

5. Number and kinds of firms in the industry

6. Major influences

   a) Business cycle

   b) Natural resources

   c) Government Regulations

   d) Business Cycle

   e) Foreign influences

B. *Market Definition*

1. Customer Profile

2. Total market size

3. Market growth

C. *Competition*

V. Products and Services

A. *Initial Products and Services*

B. *Proprietary Features*

1. Patents

2. Copyrights

3. Unique or different features

C. *Future Products and Services*

1. New products and services

BUSINESS PLAN

THE ONLINE GAME BOY STORE

January 2005

By: Judy Johnson
1620 Hillsdale
Anywhere, Colorado

TABLE OF CONTENTS

1

EXECUTIVE SUMMARY

MISSION STATEMENT

The mission of THE ONLINE GAME BOY STORE is to deliver a unique buying experience and a wide selection of products for Nintendo Game Boy enthusiasts.

BUSINESS DESCRIPTION

THE ONLINE GAME BOY STORE will be an on-line Internet e-commerce business. The products will be of high quality with great pricing. It will also have some exclusive deals for customers.

MARKETING STRATEGY

The primary objective of THE ONLINE GAME BOY STORE will be to attract customers from across the country that have an interest in Game Boy products.

A second marketing objective will be to gain repeat customers from those who use our website. This will be accomplished by providing a unique customer experience whenever someone buys from us and on-going marketing to stay in front of them.

A third marketing objective is to efficiently track where our customers are coming from and what they are buying. This is so we can continue to use the best marketing campaign for our limited dollars.

PRODUCTION PROCESS

The different products will be purchased from manufacturers, and vendors and individuals through our on-line purchasing program and through direct contact with vendors. The products will then be listed for sale on the Internet and also advertised through off-line marketing programs.

2

Shipments will be handled through the United States Postal Office. Customer service will be taken via email or by telephone.

MANAGEMENT TEAM

Mary and George Johnson will own 100% of the capital stock of the corporation. Each will own 50% of the outstanding stock. Mary Johnson is President. George Johnson is Vice President and Secretary.

OBJECTIVES OF THE TEAM

It is the objective of the team to operate the business with a minimal first year loss and to cover all start up expenses. The principals will pay themselves a minimum salary so as not to imperil the cash flow of the business.

FINANCIAL CONSIDERATION

Anticipated profits for the first years of operations are forecast as follows:

Year 1 $ (50)

Year 2 $40,150

Year 3 $96,850

Sources of the necessary funds for financing the business are as follows:

| Johnson Savings | $10,000 |
| Total Sources of Funds | $10,000 |

Anywhere State Bank will also be providing a working capital line of credit at $5,000.

INDUSTRY, MARKET AND COMPETITION

HISTORY OF THE VIDEO GAME INDUSTRY

The video game industry started in approximately 1952 with a simple tic-tac-toe game being created as a graduate essay. During the next few years, video games move into arcades and the first console game was sold in 1972. Atari in 1975 sold the first home-version of a console game with Pong as its only game. In 1980 Pac Man is sold in the United States for the first time from Japan. Microsoft enters the video game market in 1982. Nintendo releases a new faster console system in 1986 with record sales in the United States. From 1992 to 1994 the game industry starts a new chapter because of the violence in the some popular games. Mortal Kombat is so realistic that ratings are created to help parents chose games more wisely. During 1995 there are over 2 million Playstation console systems sold in the United States. The industry has continued to grow each year. In 2003, the total sales of video game consoles, games and accessories in the United States hits $7.9 billion. The industry is expected to grow again for 2004, but only by a small percentage.

Video gamers in 2004 are constantly looking for new games with faster response rates, better graphics and more networking capabilities. People are looking to play with people on-line and in computer network environments.

The main associations related with video games are:

International Game Developers Association

Entertainment and Leisure Software Publishers Association

Entertainment and Software Association

The main publications are:

GamePro Magazine – Cheats, tips, reviews and news for PC and console games

Game Revolution - online magazine for computer games and video game consoles. Includes reviews, cheats, previews, downloads, and more.

PC Zone - Britain's first and best PC games magazine is now online, featuring thousands of full games reviews, downloadable demos, cheats, competitions and chat.

Inside Games - includes news, features, columns, walkthroughs and more.

Games Radar - news, reviews, and more on the latest PC, Sony PlayStation and PS2, Sega, Microsoft Xbox, and Nintendo GameCube and Game Boy/GBA software and hardware.

MAJOR INFLUENCES

The video game industry has over 50% of the sales of consoles around the holiday season. The majority of games are also sold year-round with a spike in sales around the holiday season.

With the introduction of Mortal Kombat in 1992, the government has become more and more involved in the industry. Rating the games, started by the U.S. Senate was the first attempt to help parents chose more appropriate games for their children. We will use these changes to our advantage.

NINTENDO

Nintendo started as a playing card manufacturer. Nintendo has been developing and selling electronic video games since 1977. Since then they have sold over 1 billion video games worldwide and is a true leader in the video game industry. More than 40% of U.S. households own a Nintendo system.

We chose Nintendo and specifically Game Boy to build our business around because of two different reasons. First the systems are small, handheld games that have sold more units than other home console models. During the first year of the Game Boy Advance model release, it sold more than 4 million units. This is a huge percentage for the $1.7 billion handheld market. These units are

portable, wireless and provide quick entertainment.

Second all the new Game Boy systems have been made backward compatible for the games. This allows anyone to play any older game on a current Game Boy system. Individuals that buy these models do not have to buy a new library of games to play on their current system. There are currently over 1,000 games that can be played on the latest model of Game Boy Advance SP.

The future of Game Boy is strong. Nintendo is currently working on cables that would allow users to link up their Game Boy systems with the home console Nintendo Game Cube. This link is an uncharted area for video game manufacturers, but shows the on-going development of Game Boy within the Nintendo organization.

MARKET DEFINITION

CUSTOMER PROFILE

The primary market for THE ONLINE GAMEBOY STORE is to sell new and used Game Boy systems, games and accessories. According to NPD Group, the majority of video game players are between the ages of 13 and 44 years old. In the console type games the market is skewed towards male, with 88% being male and 12% being female. Video gaming has changed slightly over the past few years. From the Interactive Digital Software Association survey, over 60% of Americans play video games. Of that number only 43% are women and the average age of gamers being 28 years old.

This creates Online Game Boy Store's Customer Profile:

Male

Between 13-30 years old

Mid to upper income bracket homes ($40,000+)

TOTAL MARKET SIZE

According to the Entertainment Software Association, over 50% of all Americans play video games. But 97% of people who purchase games are 18 years of age or older. In people under 18 years old, over 83% get their parents permission before they buy a game. Only 43% of purchasers are men, while 57% are women. Women do not play as often as men, but they do buy more games than men.

The following chart shows the video game sales for the past few years:

2001	$6.35 billion in sales
2002	$6.9 billion in sales
2003	$7.0 billion in sales

During 2003, the sales of console games included over $5.8 billion, while computer games contributed $1.2 billion.

Here is the breakdown of types of games sold:

54% were rated "E" for Everyone

30.5% were rated "T" for Teen

11.9% were rated "M" for Mature

Over 70% of the top 20 best-selling games for consoles were rated either "E" or "T".

Top Video Game Sales by # of Units Sold

Action games	27.1%
Sports	17.6%
Racing	15.7%
Roleplaying	8.7%

MARKET GROWTH

According to the Entertainment Software Association (ESA), the video game industry in the United

States has grown from $3.0 billion in sales in 1996 to over $7.9 billion in 2003. In addition, the number of units sold has increased from 84.6 million in 1996 to 239 million units in 2003. During the next few years, analysts expect the market to level off to a little over $8 billion in sales.

COMPETITION

As the Internet starts to come around again, more and more people are buying on-line. Per Shop.org's report on the "State of Retailing Online 7.0", there were over $114 billion in sales online during 2003. This was up 51% from the year prior. Early estimate for 2004 has also shown an increase in online sales during 2004. Most analysts predict the trend will continue to increase for on-line purchases.

EBGames.com: This online and offline retailer focuses on all console games including Playstation 2, Xbox, Gamecube, Game boy and Nintendo DS. They sell hardware, games, in both new and used formats.

Half.com: This site is an eBay site that sells both new and used games and hardware for all systems, in addition to Books, Textbooks, Movies, DVDs, computers and software and other electronics.

VGfanatic.com: This is a smaller site compared to the above two. This site also supports many different video game platforms. They sell both new and used games and have an online service to buy used games. It is a great model for creating a process around buying games. When someone sells a game to VGfanatic.com they can receive a better price if chose to receive credit with VGfanatic.com instead of cash/check. This is also a strategy that we will incorporate into our business.

Bizrate.com & eBay.com and Other Auction sites: Auction sites would be considered competition because anyone can list on these sites. All of these sites will need to be monitored on an on-going basis because they change so often.

8

It is anticipated that additional competition will come into the market as new Internet e-commerce companies are formed and as more people learn to use the online auction sites.

COMPETITION STRENGTHS AND WEAKNESSES

Competitive Strengths

1. HALF.COM and EBGAMES.COM are the largest competitors. They have the most visitors coming to their sites. Per Alexa.com, HALF.COM through eBay receives approximately 1% of all of eBay's site traffic (over 1 million visitors per month) EBGAMES.COM has approximately 15,000 visitors per month to their site. EBGAMES.COM also has brick and mortar stores where they can advertise their website.

2. VGFANATIC.COM is the smallest of the competitors, but the most targeted. The traffic counts for VGFANATIC.COM are too small to be listed on Alexa.com.

3. OTHER AUCTION SITES pose a competitive threat and a strength for THE ONLINE GAME BOY STORE. Being proficient in using the auction sites will help to grow the business without spending too much on advertising and infrastructure.

Competitive Weaknesses

1. Neither of the large competitors have the ability to move quickly when the market pricing changes. This will allow THE ONLINE GAME BOY STORE to take advantage of higher pricing opportunities and deliver exactly what our customers want.

2. All of the competitors carry all the different consoles. The inventory needs for their sites is much larger than that for THE ONLINE GAME BOY STORE. THE ONLINE GAME BOY STORE will have reduced expenses because they do not have to carry all the different systems.

PRODUCTS AND SERVICES

INITIAL PRODUCTS

<u>New Game Boy Handhelds (Hardware)</u>
 SP (Special Project)
 New Handhelds as they become available

<u>Used Game Boy Handhelds (Hardware)</u>
 Color
 SP (Special Project)

<u>New Game Boy Games (Software)</u>

<u>BanjoPilot</u>
Released: Jan 11, 2005

<u>The Legend of Zelda: The Minish Cap</u>
Released: Jan 10, 2005
<u>Blades of Thunder</u>
Released: Dec 21, 2004
<u>Kingdom Hearts: Chain of Memories</u>
Released: Dec 07, 2004
<u>Final Fantasy I & II: Dawn of Souls</u>
Released: Nov 29, 2004

<u>Used Game Boy Games (Software)</u>
There are currently over 1,000 game titles available for the latest Game Boy system

Game Title	Category	ESRB Rating	Release Date	Publisher
Disney/Pixar's The Incredibles	Action	E	Nov 02, 2004	THQ
Pokémon LeafGreen	RPG	E	Sep 09, 2004	Nintendo
Pokémon FireRed	RPG	E	Sep 09, 2004	Nintendo
SpongeBob SquarePants Movie, The	Action	E	Oct 2004	THQ
Shrek 2 (GBA)	Action	E	May 04, 2004	Activision
Namco Museum (GBA)	Arcade	E	Jun 11, 2001	Namco
Midnight Club Racing	Racing	E	Nov 05, 2001	Destination Software
Kirby & The Amazing Mirror	Action, Adventure	E	Oct 18, 2004	Nintendo
Cartoon Network Block Party	Board Games	E	Aug 03, 2004	Majesco Sales Inc.
Shrek 2: Beg For Mercy!	Action	E	Oct 25, 2004	Activision

PROPRIETARY OR UNIQUE FEATURES

Since THE ONLINE GAME BOY STORE will focus on only the Game Boy systems and games, we will be able to build up a clientele within a very focused niche. This niche will allow us to offer additional newsletters about games, news, products and hidden tips and game techniques. One of the biggest factors that will separate us from our competition is that we will be very vocal with parents about our role in the video game industry.

MARKETING PLAN

OVERVIEW

THE ONLINE GAME BOY STORE   is going to be a highly targeted website for Game Boy enthusiasts. We will be using both online and offline marketing. We need to focus on not only selling used Game Boy games, but also buying them as well. We have contacted the manufacturer of older games and have picked up a selection of older games on an on-going basis.

The biggest issue we will have in marketing is making sure Game Boy enthusiasts are aware of our services. To create awareness we will position ourselves as the Game Boy Expert. We will become involved in the gaming industry through sponsoring local tournaments and events, holding warehouse sales with large discounts, participating in radio and TV interviews and having a very active web presence. We will become very vocal on violence in video games and use that to get more media exposure. We will be the Experts for interviews whenever a new game, console or issue comes out about the gaming industry.

MARKETING OBJECTIVES

The primary objective of THE GAME BOY STORE will be to attract customers from across the country that have an interest in Game Boy products.

A second marketing objective will be to gain repeat customers from those who use our website. This will be accomplished by providing a unique customer experience whenever someone buys from us.

A third marketing objective is to efficiently track where our customers are coming from. This is so we can continue to use the best marketing campaign for our limited dollars.

MARKETING STRATEGY-ADVERTISING AND PROMOTION

OBJECTIVE #1

To achieve Objective #1, we will need to find creative ways to get in front of our customers. To do this we will use online and offline marketing methods attracting people to our website.

OFFLINE METHODS

Local events will be held in conjunction with other kid-friendly events. We will start in our home town testing different events and then roll out to a national level with the ones that had the largest impact.

Becoming the **Game Boy Expert** does not happen overnight. We will start out by faxing a press release to radio stations across the country on video gaming topics especially related to Game Boy. Next we will talk with local kid's club about proper use of video games and appropriate games for each age group. Adults and kids will look to us for the latest in gaming news.

We will also be setting up **speaking engagements** at different events like:

Kid's Expo

Women's Expo

Mother's Workshops

Community Education – teach parents about safe use of video games

Parent's Expo

Club Memberships will also be used to get more prospects on our database. Individuals can sign up for memberships without a cost to get news, information and product updates.

ONLINE METHODS

A very strong web presence will be key to our success. Our website will be designed to be **easy for kids and adults to use**. We will have the ability to buy or sell games using the latest (and easiest) in online shopping carts. In addition we will have a sign up on our site for a monthly newsletter on Game Boy products, new game releases, game developer interviews and other special sale items.

The website will also use the **appropriate keywords** in the meta tags (what search engine look at) and throughout the body of the written content. This will help to get us a higher unpaid placement in the search engine results. Keywords from Overture.com for December 2004 for Game Boy are listed below. You can see by the following chart which words are searched more heavily than others and what the top bid is for purchased pay-per-click advertising. These are words that we will use in our site.

	Keyword	Search Volume	Top Bid	
☐	game boy	279,359	0.35	Bid Tool
☐	game boy advance	117,088	0.49	Bid Tool
☐	game boy ds	51,218	0.13	Bid Tool
☐	game boy advance sp	49,788	0.26	Bid Tool
☐	game boy advance rom	30,543	No Bids	
☐	game boy advance game	29,771	0.21	Bid Tool
☐	game boy game	27,411	0.61	Bid Tool
☐	game boy sp	24,257	0.25	Bid Tool
☐	game boy advanced	18,182	0.24	Bid Tool
☐	game boy rom	15,887	0.11	Bid Tool
☐	game boy cheat	15,145	No Bids	
☐	cheap game boy advance	13,401	0.12	Bid Tool
☐	game boy color	11,196	0.35	Bid Tool

In addition to our website, we will also utilize the **online auction sites**, eBay.com, Amazon.com, Bizrate.com and Nextag.com. This strategy allows us to collect email addresses of individuals that are interested or have purchased Game Boy items from us. This strategy increases our customer list all the time.

Advertising will consist of **writing articles** for online ezines (electronic newsletters) like:

       www.game-players.net

       www.amf.com

       www.nintendo.com

And parenting ezines like:

       www.empoweredparent.com

       www.home-and-family.com

       www.kidscentralstation.com

Finally we will use the affiliate model for increasing traffic to our site. If another vendor signs up for our affiliate program we will pay them commissions for any sales made through our website. The www.1shoppingcart.com has an affiliate tracking module so we will not have to track this manually.

OBJECTIVE #2

To achieve Objective #2, we have an on-going marketing campaign with sales offers and unique tips, tricks and information that we will continually provide to our customers. We will "touch" our current customers over 12 times per year with different items through emails and direct mail. Being constantly "in front" of our customers makes us the first choice when they go to buy a game. We will also use a set of rewards to get them to buy more from us.

OBJECTIVE #3

To achieve Objective #3 and since we are a new company and a small one, we need to use our marketing and advertising dollars effectively. To do that we will keep track of all marketing campaigns to see which ones generated more sales.

Since most of our customers will initially come from the Internet and people that hear us speak on the radio, we will need some way to track where these people come from. One way we will do that is to have different landing pages for the different campaigns. When we are being interviewed on a radio show, we will have people visit our site: www.gameboystore.com. The website we will use when the come from the Internet will be www.gameboycentral.com. We will then be able to track where the visitors heard about our online store. Tracking customers is a major marketing objective.

When we have customers we need a good database to be able to continue to send marketing messages to them. The database will be kept in the online shopping cart. After careful review of popular shopping carts, we have decided to have www.1shoppingcart.com provide the shopping cart services. With this package, we have lots of tools to use in sending out messages to our customers.

PRICING

Pricing will go with the market trends. Newer and more popular games will be priced higher than older games. We will be pricing our products at the top of the price range because we will be adding in Free bonus gifts that clients can not get elsewhere.

In our buying process, we will be able to negotiate better pricing because we will become a leader in sales for Game Boy products.

Online we will "pay" more for used games where the client will be willing to take a credit with THE GAME BOY STORE instead of cash/check. We will do this because it is cheaper to give them credit than to cut manual checks. The use of PayPal will be researched at a later date for making payments.

<u>SALES</u>

All sales will be made by major credit card taken ONLY through www.1shoppingcart.com. Credit cards from VISA, MASTER CARD, AMERICAN EXPRESS, and DISCOVER will be accepted. Checks and money orders will not be accepted.

The majority of sales will be conducted through the shopping cart on the website. In addition, we will have different promotions to up-sell the customers other products as an automatic function I the shopping cart system.

THE PRODUCTION PLAN

FACILITY REQUIREMENTS

The GAME BOY STORE will not need very much space for the first couple of years. We estimate we will need approximately 500 square feet, which we have found in a local office building for $500 per month.

The building has high speed Internet running into the building already. UPS already picks up at this location also.

EQUIPMENT REQUIREMENTS

The equipment needs are minimal. Equipment needs include:

2 Computers	$2,000
Printer/copier/fax combo	$ 500
Shelving	$ 200
Phone	$ 200
Fax	$ 100
4-Drawer Filing Cabinets	$ 150
2 Desks & chairs	$ 500
Total Expenses	**$3,650**

Our Online Service Providers are as follows with appropriate monthly fees:

Host4Profit (hosting)	$29
1shoppingcart.com (online shopping cart)	$69
Authorize.net (gateway)	$20
Nova (merchant card services)	$50
Total Monthly Internet Fees	**$168**

Website Development

The initial website development will be handled by George Johnson. Some of the customized work will be outsourced by receiving the best bid using www.elance.com. Since George has studied website design and development, he will oversee all changes to the website.

LABOR REQUIREMENTS

The two principals will each operate the different sides of the business while working together. George Johnson will mainly be in charge of buying Game Boy hardware and software, including managing inventory levels. Mary Johnson will be responsible for the selling side of the Game Boy business, including shipping. The two will work together to make sure they are continually buying what people what to buy from THE ONLINE GAME BOY STORE. Both will be heavily involved in the marketing and financial side of the business.

As the business expands we will add staff as necessary. As the time spent on shipping becomes more and more, we predict we will need a part-time high school student to help with the process.

The following employees and their projected monthly salaries are as follows:

Buy Side of Business	George Johnson	$1,500
Sell Side of Business	Mary Johnson	1,500
TOTAL LABOR		**$3,000**

SALES PROCESS

As any Internet business must do, it must manage its ongoing website content, inventory and sales. First, the items for sale on the site will be handled through www.1shoppingcart.com. The

shopping cart has features to measure inventory and make sure we do not sell more than we have in stock. It also manages shipping charges and necessary taxes and has sales reports for shipping.

George will be responsible for adding items to the shopping cart when he purchases them from a vendor or individual. He must not only add each item to the shopping cart but also to the appropriate pages of the website.

Once someone has purchased an item through the website, Mary will receive an email of the sale. The sales report can then be printed off in addition to the appropriate shipping labels. Mary will then box up the items and take the packages to the post office. When the number of packages is over 15, the post office will do special pickups.

Reconciliation of the bank accounts will initially be George's responsibility. Both Mary and George will review on a weekly basis the updates to the website and on-going marketing.

CUSTOMER SERVICE PROCESS

Customer service will be handled through email support and telephone support. Mary will be responsible for customer support. All calls will be initially logged into Microsoft Excel so that a knowledge base of questions can be developed in the future.

MANAGEMENT TEAM AND KEY PERSONNEL

Mary and George Johnson have filed the appropriate papers with the state for a limited liability corporation under the name of THE ONLINE GAME BOY STORE. Mary is the president while George is vice president and secretary. Each has 50% of the capital stock of the corporation.

George and Mary expect to work 40 hours a week until the operation can afford additional staffing. After the business has grown a couple of part-time employees will be hired. This business can be run from almost anywhere.

The company's attorneys, Solie, Johnson and Johnson Ltd. together with their Certified Public Accounting Firm of Holland and Webber have recommended that THE ONLINE GAME BOY STORE be set up as a Limited Liability Corporation for Internal Revenue reporting purposes.

The business has been filed under the laws of the State of Minnesota with the effective date being January 5, 2005.

BUSINESS ADVISORS

The following business advisors have been or will be used as needed:

Accountant:	Judy Holland with Holland and Webber, Certified Public Accountants, Anywhere, MN
Lawyer:	Karen Solie with Solie, Johnson and Johnson Ltd., Minneapolis, MN
Banker:	Adam Johnston, President of Anywhere State Bank, Anywhere, MN
Insurance:	Emily Marshall with Marshall Insurance, Anywhere, MN
Advertising:	Marsha Forester of Forester and Forester Advertising Agency, Eagan, MN

THE FINANCIAL PLAN

SUMMARY

Taking into consideration that THE ONLINE GAME BOY STORE will be a new Internet storefront, conservative accounting procedures and projections have been made. The following Income Projections are as follows for the first three years of operations of the store:

	Profit/Loss
YEAR 1-	$ 4,890
YEAR 2-	$40,800
YEAR 3-	$97,500

Income Statement projections indicate that the store will have a positive cash flow beginning with the twelfth month of operations. At that time it is forecast that monthly cash receipts will amount to $26,400 with expenses of $4,425. Until that time, the line of credit from the Anywhere State Bank and the Johnson's investment should be sufficient to provide the store with its necessary cash needs. The line of credit may be used during the months of May through October. If cash flow needs change, Mary and George may have to take their salary the following month. The income projections almost match the cash flow statements because since all items are paid for online the cash comes in and goes out basically during the same month.

The three year balance sheet projects indicate that the net worth (Owner's Equity) of THE ONLINE GAME BOY STORE will be as follows:

YEAR 1- $950

YEAR 2- $41,150

YEAR 3-$97,850

The three year projections for INCOME STATEMENTS, CASH FLOW and BALANCE

SHEETS are shown on the following pages.

Each of these spreadsheets has been prepared by the firm of Holland and Webber, Certified Public Accountants located in Anywhere, N.C. All of the cost information is supported by documented:

* Vendor and Supplier Cost Proposals

* Contractor Bids

* Local Wage and Salary Schedules

* Public Utility Estimates

* Letters of Financial Commitments

* Forester and Forester Advertising Proposal

* Bear and Marshall Insurance Estimate

SOURCES AND USES OF FUNDS

Cash from the Johnson's Savings and sale of some of their common stock	$10,000
Total Start-Up Funds	$10,000
Start Up Expenses	$ 3,850

The Anywhere State Bank has also agreed to provide THE ONLINE GAME BOY STORE with a line of credit amounting to $5,000 should it be necessary.

Year 1 Income Statement Projections for THE ONLINE GAME BOY STORE

	Price/Cost	January	February	March	April	May	June	July	August	Sept	Oct	Nov	Dec	Totals
Number of Customers per Month														
New Hardware Sales		5	10	10	10	20	20	20	20	40	60	80	80	340
Used Hardware Sales		10	20	20	20	40	40	40	40	80	120	160	160	
New Game Sales		20	40	40	40	80	80	80	80	130	200	250	250	1,290
Used Game Sales		20	40	40	40	80	80	80	80	130	200	250	250	1,290
Revenues	**Price**													
New Hardware Sales	$ 85	425	850	850	850	1,700	1,700	1,700	1,700	3,400	5,100	6,800	6,800	
Used Hardware Sales	$ 60	600	1,200	1,200	1,200	2,400	2,400	2,400	2,400	4,800	7,200	9,600	9,600	
New Game Sales	$ 30	600	1,200	1,200	1,200	2,400	2,400	2,400	2,400	3,900	6,000	7,500	7,500	
Used Game Sales	$ 10	200	400	400	400	800	800	800	800	1,300	2,000	2,500	2,500	
Total Revenues		1,825	3,650	3,650	3,650	7,300	7,300	7,300	7,300	13,400	20,300	26,400	26,400	$ 128,475
Cost of Goods	**Cost**													
New Hardware Sales	$ 45	225	450	450	450	900	900	900	900	1,800	2,700	3,600	3,600	
Used Hardware Sales	$ 50	500	1,000	1,000	1,000	2,000	2,000	2,000	2,000	4,000	6,000	8,000	8,000	
New Game Sales	$ 14	280	560	560	560	1,120	1,120	1,120	1,120	1,820	2,800	3,500	3,500	
Used Game Sales	$ 5	100	200	200	200	400	400	400	400	650	1,000	1,250	1,250	
Total COGS		1,105	2,210	2,210	2,210	4,420	4,420	4,420	4,420	8,270	12,500	16,350	16,350	$ 78,885
Expenses														
Fixed Expenses														
Insurance		250												250
Rent		500	500	500	500	500	500	500	500	500	500	500	500	6,000
Interest - Loan		-	-	-	-	-	-	-	-	-	-	-	4,740	4,740
Interest - Mortgage		-	-	-	-	-	-	-	-	-	-	-	200	200
Variable Expenses														-
Salaries		-	-	-	3,000	3,000	3,000	3,000	3,000	3,000	3,000	3,000	3,000	27,000
Advertising		500	500	500	500	500	500	500	500	500	500	500	500	6,000
Dues & Subscriptions		100	-	-	-	-	-	-	-	-	-	-	-	100
Legal & Accounting		250	-	-	-	-	-	-	-	-	-	-	-	250
Office Supplies		25	25	25	25	25	25	25	25	25	25	25	25	300
Telephone		50	50	50	50	50	50	50	50	50	50	50	50	600
Utilities		100	100	100	100	100	100	100	100	100	100	100	100	1,200
Website Fees		250	250	250	250	250	250	250	250	250	250	250	250	3,000
Total Expenses		2,025	1,425	1,425	4,425	4,425	4,425	4,425	4,425	4,425	4,425	4,425	9,365	49,640
Net Profit		(1,305)	15	15	(2,985)	(1,545)	(1,545)	(1,545)	(1,545)	705	3,375	5,625	685	$ (50)
Cumulative Profit		(1,305)	(1,290)	(1,275)	(4,260)	(5,805)	(7,350)	(8,895)	(10,440)	(9,735)	(6,360)	(735)	(50)	0%

Year 2 Income Statement Projections for THE ONLINE GAME BOY STORE

	Price/Cost	January	February	March	April	May	June	July	August	Sept	Oct	Nov	Dec	Totals
Number of Customers per Month														
New Hardware Sales		50	50	50	70	70	70	60	60	60	60	300	300	980
Used Hardware Sales		250	250	250	200	200	200	150	150	150	150	100	100	
New Game Sales		300	300	150	150	150	150	200	200	200	200	500	500	3,000
Used Game Sales		300	300	150	150	150	150	200	200	200	200	500	500	3,000
Revenues	**Price**													
New Hardware Sales	$ 85	$ 4,250	$ 4,250	$ 4,250	$ 5,950	$ 5,950	$ 5,950	$ 5,100	$ 5,100	$ 5,100	$ 5,100	$ 25,500	$ 25,500	
Used Hardware Sales	$ 60	$ 15,000	$ 15,000	$ 15,000	$ 12,000	$ 12,000	$ 12,000	$ 9,000	$ 9,000	$ 9,000	$ 9,000	$ 6,000	$ 6,000	
New Game Sales	$ 30	$ 9,000	$ 9,000	$ 4,500	$ 4,500	$ 4,500	$ 4,500	$ 6,000	$ 6,000	$ 6,000	$ 6,000	$ 15,000	$ 15,000	
Used Game Sales	$ 10	$ 3,000	$ 3,000	$ 1,500	$ 1,500	$ 1,500	$ 1,500	$ 2,000	$ 2,000	$ 2,000	$ 2,000	$ 5,000	$ 5,000	
Total Revenues		$ 31,250	$ 31,250	$ 25,250	$ 23,950	$ 23,950	$ 23,950	$ 22,100	$ 22,100	$ 22,100	$ 22,100	$ 51,500	$ 51,500	$ 351,000
Cost of Goods	**Cost**													
New Hardware Sales	$ 45	$ 2,250	$ 2,250	$ 2,250	$ 3,150	$ 3,150	$ 3,150	$ 2,700	$ 2,700	$ 2,700	$ 2,700	$ 13,500	$ 13,500	
Used Hardware Sales	$ 50	$ 12,500	$ 12,500	$ 12,500	$ 10,000	$ 10,000	$ 10,000	$ 7,500	$ 7,500	$ 7,500	$ 7,500	$ 5,000	$ 5,000	
New Game Sales	$ 14	$ 4,200	$ 4,200	$ 2,100	$ 2,100	$ 2,100	$ 2,100	$ 2,800	$ 2,800	$ 2,800	$ 2,800	$ 7,000	$ 7,000	
Used Game Sales	$ 5	$ 1,500	$ 1,500	$ 750	$ 750	$ 750	$ 750	$ 1,000	$ 1,000	$ 1,000	$ 1,000	$ 2,500	$ 2,500	
Total COGS		$ 20,450	$ 20,450	$ 17,600	$ 16,000	$ 16,000	$ 16,000	$ 14,000	$ 14,000	$ 14,000	$ 14,000	$ 28,000	$ 28,000	$ 218,500
Expenses														
Fixed Expenses														
Insurance		$ 250												$ 250
Rent		$ 500	500	500	500	500	500	500	500	500	500	500	500	$ 6,000
Interest - Loan		$ -	-	-	-	-	-	-	-	-	-	-	-	$ -
Interest - Mortgage		$ -	-	-	-	-	-	-	-	-	-	-	-	$ -
Variable Expenses														
Salaries		$ 6,000	6,000	6,000	6,000	6,000	6,000	6,000	6,000	6,000	6,000	6,000	6,000	$ 72,000
Advertising		$ 500	500	500	500	500	500	500	500	500	500	500	500	$ 6,000
Dues & Subscriptions		$ 100	-	-	-	-	-	-	-	-	-	-	-	$ 100
Legal & Accounting		$ -	-	900	-	-	-	-	-	-	-	-	-	$ 900
Office Supplies		$ 25	25	25	25	25	2,025	25	25	25	25	25	25	$ 2,300
Telephone		$ 50	50	50	50	50	50	50	50	50	50	50	50	$ 600
Utilities		$ 100	100	100	100	100	100	100	100	100	100	100	100	$ 1,200
Website Fees		$ 250	250	250	250	250	250	250	250	250	250	250	250	$ 3,000
Total Expenses		$ 7,775	7,425	8,325	7,425	7,425	9,425	7,425	7,425	7,425	7,425	7,425	7,425	$ 92,350
Net Profit		$ 3,025	3,375	(675)	525	525	(1,475)	675	675	675	675	16,075	16,075	$ 40,150
Cumulative Profit		$ 3,025	6,400	5,725	6,250	6,775	5,300	5,975	6,650	7,325	8,000	24,075	40,150	11%

Year 3 Income Statement Projections for THE ONLINE GAME BOY STORE

	Price/Cost	January	February	March	April	May	June	July	August	Sept	Oct	Nov	Dec	Totals
Number of Customers per Month														
New Hardware Sales		100	100	80	80	80	80	80	70	70	70	500	500	1,450
Used Hardware Sales		300	300	150	150	150	150	150	150	150	150	200	200	
New Game Sales		600	600	500	500	500	500	500	500	500	500	800	800	6,800
Used Game Sales		600	600	500	500	500	500	500	500	500	500	800	800	6,800
Revenues	Price													
New Hardware Sales	$ 85	8,500	8,500	6,800	6,800	6,800	6,800	6,800	5,950	5,950	5,950	42,500	42,500	
Used Hardware Sales	$ 60	18,000	18,000	9,000	9,000	9,000	9,000	9,000	9,000	9,000	9,000	12,000	12,000	
New Game Sales	$ 30	18,000	18,000	15,000	15,000	15,000	15,000	15,000	15,000	15,000	15,000	24,000	24,000	
Used Game Sales	$ 10	6,000	6,000	5,000	5,000	5,000	5,000	5,000	5,000	5,000	5,000	8,000	8,000	
Total Revenues		$ 50,500	$ 50,500	$ 35,800	$ 35,800	$ 35,800	$ 35,800	$ 35,800	$ 34,950	$ 34,950	$ 34,950	$ 86,500	$ 86,500	$ 557,850
Cost of Goods	Cost													
New Hardware Sales	$ 45	4,500	4,500	3,600	3,600	3,600	3,600	3,600	3,150	3,150	3,150	22,500	22,500	
Used Hardware Sales	$ 50	15,000	15,000	7,500	7,500	7,500	7,500	7,500	7,500	7,500	7,500	10,000	10,000	
New Game Sales	$ 14	8,400	8,400	7,000	7,000	7,000	7,000	7,000	7,000	7,000	7,000	11,200	11,200	
Used Game Sales	$ 5	3,000	3,000	2,500	2,500	2,500	2,500	2,500	2,500	2,500	2,500	4,000	4,000	
Total COGS		$ 30,900	$ 30,900	$ 20,600	$ 20,600	$ 20,600	$ 20,600	$ 20,600	$ 20,150	$ 20,150	$ 20,150	$ 47,700	$ 47,700	$ 320,650
Expenses														
Fixed Expenses														
Insurance		$ 250												$ 250
Rent		500	500	500	500	500	500	500	500	500	500	500	500	6,000
Interest - Loan		-	-	-	-	-	-	-	-	-	-	-	-	-
Interest - Mortgage		-	-	-	-	-	-	-	-	-	-	-	-	-
Variable Expenses														
Salaries		10,000	10,000	10,000	10,000	10,000	10,000	10,000	10,000	10,000	10,000	10,000	10,000	120,000
Advertising		500	500	500	500	500	500	500	500	500	500	500	500	6,000
Dues & Subscriptions		100	-	-	-	-	-	-	-	-	-	-	-	100
Legal & Accounting		-	-	900	-	-	-	-	-	-	-	-	-	900
Office Supplies		25	25	25	25	25	2,025	25	25	25	25	25	25	2,300
Telephone		50	50	50	50	50	50	50	50	50	50	50	50	600
Utilities		100	100	100	100	100	100	100	100	100	100	100	100	1,200
Website Fees		250	250	250	250	250	250	250	250	250	250	250	250	3,000
Total Expenses		$ 11,775	$ 11,425	$ 12,325	$ 11,425	$ 11,425	$ 13,425	$ 11,425	$ 11,425	$ 11,425	$ 11,425	$ 11,425	$ 11,425	$ 140,350
Net Profit		$ 7,825	$ 8,175	$ 2,875	$ 3,775	$ 3,775	$ 1,775	$ 3,775	$ 3,375	$ 3,375	$ 3,375	$ 27,375	$ 27,375	$ 96,850
Cumulative Profit		$ 7,825	16,000	18,875	22,650	26,425	28,200	31,975	35,350	38,725	42,100	69,475	96,850	17%

THE ONLINE GAME BOY STORE

Pro-Forma Balance Sheet

Start-Up

ASSETS

Cash	$	6,500
Inventories	$	-
Property	$	-
Equipment	$	3,500
Total Assets	**$**	**10,000**

LIABILITIES AND OWNER'S EQUITY

Account Payables	$	-
Anywhere Bank Loan	$	-
Anywhere Mortgage	$	-
Loan from Shareholders	$	9,000
Total Liabilities	**$**	**9,000**
Retained Earnings	$	-
Common Stock	$	1,000
Total Owner's Equity	**$**	**1,000**
Total Liabilities and Owner's Equity	**$**	**10,000**

THE ONLINE GAME BOY STORE

Pro-Forma Balance Sheet

End of Year 1

ASSETS

Cash	$	10,390
Inventories	$	5,376
Property	$	-
Equipment	$	3,000
Total Assets	**$**	**18,766**

LIABILITIES AND OWNER'S EQUITY

Account Payables	$	8,816
Anywhere Bank Loan	$	-
Anywhere Mortgage	$	-
Loan from Shareholders	$	9,000
Total Liabilities	**$**	**17,816**
Retained Earnings	$	(50)
Common Stock	$	1,000
Total Owner's Equity	**$**	**950**
Total Liabilities and Owner's Equity	**$**	**18,766**

THE ONLINE GAME BOY STORE

Pro-Forma Balance Sheet

End of Year 2

ASSETS

Cash	$	52,540
Inventories	$	2,358
Property	$	-
Equipment	$	4,000
Total Assets	**$**	**58,898**

LIABILITIES AND OWNER'S EQUITY

Account Payables	$	8,748
Anywhere Bank Loan	$	-
Anywhere Mortgage	$	-
Loan from Shareholders	$	9,000
Total Liabilities	**$**	**17,748**
Retained Earnings	$	40,150
Common Stock	$	1,000
Total Owner's Equity	**$**	**41,150**
Total Liabilities and Owner's Equity	**$**	**58,898**

THE ONLINE GAME BOY STORE

Pro-Forma Balance Sheet

End of Year 3

ASSETS

Cash	$	151,390
Inventories	$	7,328
Property	$	-
Equipment	$	6,000
Total Assets	**$**	**164,718**

LIABILITIES AND OWNER'S EQUITY

Account Payables	$	57,868
Anywhere Bank Loan	$	-
Anywhere Mortgage	$	-
Loan from Shareholders	$	9,000
Total Liabilities	**$**	**66,868**
Retained Earnings	$	96,850
Common Stock	$	1,000
Total Owner's Equity	**$**	**97,850**
Total Liabilities and Owner's Equity	**$**	**164,718**

Year 1 Cash Flow Projections for THE ONLINE GAME BOY STORE

	Price	Start Up	January	February	March	April	May	June	July	August	Sept	Oct	Nov	Dec	Totals
Beginning Cash		$ 10,000	$ 5,200	$ 4,395	$ 4,410	$ 4,425	$ 1,440	$ -	$ -	$ -	$ -	$ 705	$ 4,080	$ 9,705	
Number of Customers per Month															
New Hardware Sales			5	10	10	10	20	20	20	20	40	60	80	80	340
Used Hardware Sales			10	20	20	20	40	40	40	40	80	120	160	160	
New Game Sales			20	40	40	40	80	80	80	80	130	200	250	250	1,290
Used Game Sales			20	40	40	40	80	80	80	80	130	200	250	250	1,290
Revenues															
New Hardware Sales	$ 85		425	850	850	850	1,700	1,700	1,700	1,700	3,400	5,100	6,800	6,800	
Used Hardware Sales	$ 60		600	1,200	1,200	1,200	2,400	2,400	2,400	2,400	4,800	7,200	9,600	9,600	
New Game Sales	$ 30		600	1,200	1,200	1,200	2,400	2,400	2,400	2,400	3,900	6,000	7,500	7,500	
Used Game Sales	$ 10		200	400	400	400	800	800	800	800	1,300	2,000	2,500	2,500	
Total Revenues		$ -	$ 1,825	$ 3,650	$ 3,650	$ 3,650	$ 7,300	$ 7,300	$ 7,300	$ 7,300	$ 13,400	$ 20,300	$ 26,400	$ 26,400	$ 128,475
Total COGS			$ 1,105	$ 2,210	$ 2,210	$ 2,210	$ 4,420	$ 4,420	$ 4,420	$ 4,420	$ 8,270	$ 12,500	$ 16,350	$ 16,350	$ 78,885
Expenses															
Purchases		$ 3,500	$ -	$ -	$ -	$ -	$ -	$ -	$ -	$ -	$ -	$ -	$ -	$ 4,740	$ 4,740
Insurance		$ 250	-	-	-	-	-	-	-	-	-	-	-	200	200
Rent		$ -	500	500	500	500	500	500	500	500	500	500	500	500	6,000
Interest - Loan			-	-	-	-	-	-	-	-	-	-	-	-	-
Interest - Mortgage			-	-	-	-	-	-	-	-	-	-	-	-	-
Salaries			-	-	-	3,000	3,000	3,000	3,000	3,000	3,000	3,000	3,000	3,000	27,000
Advertising			500	500	500	500	500	500	500	500	500	500	500	500	6,000
Dues & Subscriptions		$ 200	100	-	-	-	-	-	-	-	-	-	-	-	100
Legal & Accounting		$ 150	-	-	-	-	-	-	-	-	-	-	-	-	-
Office Supplies		$ 200	25	25	25	25	25	25	25	25	25	25	25	25	300
Telephone			50	50	50	50	50	50	50	50	50	50	50	50	600
Utilities			100	100	100	100	100	100	100	100	100	100	100	100	1,200
Website Fees		$ 500	250	250	250	250	250	250	250	250	250	250	250	250	3,000
Total Expenses		$ 4,800	$ 1,525	$ 1,425	$ 1,425	$ 4,425	$ 4,425	$ 4,425	$ 4,425	$ 4,425	$ 4,425	$ 4,425	$ 4,425	$ 9,365	$ 49,140
Ending Cash		$ 5,200	$ 4,395	$ 4,410	$ 4,425	$ 1,440	$ (105)	$ (1,545)	$ (1,545)	$ (1,545)	$ 705	$ 4,080	$ 9,705	$ 10,390	
Line Of Credit Used							$ 105	$ 1,545	$ 1,545	$ 1,545					$ 4,740

Year 2 Cash Flow Projections for THE ONLINE GAME BOY STORE

	Price/Cost	January	February	March	April	May	June	July	August	Sept	Oct	Nov	Dec	Totals
Beginning Cash		$ 10,390	$ 13,415	$ 16,790	$ 16,115	$ 16,640	$ 17,165	$ 17,690	$ 18,365	$ 19,040	$ 19,715	$ 20,390	$ 36,465	
Number of Customers per Month														
Revenues	**Price**													
New Hardware Sales	$ 85	$ 4,250	$ 4,250	$ 4,250	$ 5,950	$ 5,950	$ 5,950	$ 5,100	$ 5,100	$ 5,100	$ 5,100	$ 25,500	$ 25,500	
Used Hardware Sales	$ 60	15,000	15,000	15,000	12,000	12,000	12,000	9,000	9,000	9,000	9,000	6,000	6,000	
New Game Sales	$ 30	9,000	9,000	4,500	4,500	4,500	4,500	6,000	6,000	6,000	6,000	15,000	15,000	
Used Game Sales	$ 10	3,000	3,000	1,500	1,500	1,500	1,500	2,000	2,000	2,000	2,000	5,000	5,000	
Total Revenues		$ 31,250	$ 31,250	$ 25,250	$ 23,950	$ 23,950	$ 23,950	$ 22,100	$ 22,100	$ 22,100	$ 22,100	$ 51,500	$ 51,500	$ 351,000
Cost of Goods	**Cost**													
New Hardware Sales	$ 45	$ 2,250	$ 2,250	$ 2,250	$ 3,150	$ 3,150	$ 3,150	$ 2,700	$ 2,700	$ 2,700	$ 2,700	$ 13,500	$ 13,500	
Used Hardware Sales	$ 50	12,500	12,500	12,500	10,000	10,000	10,000	7,500	7,500	7,500	7,500	5,000	5,000	
New Game Sales	$ 14	4,200	4,200	2,100	2,100	2,100	2,100	2,800	2,800	2,800	2,800	7,000	7,000	
Used Game Sales	$ 5	1,500	1,500	750	750	750	750	1,000	1,000	1,000	1,000	2,500	2,500	
Total COGS		$ 20,450	$ 20,450	$ 17,600	$ 16,000	$ 16,000	$ 16,000	$ 14,000	$ 14,000	$ 14,000	$ 14,000	$ 28,000	$ 28,000	$ 218,500
Expenses														
Purchases		$ -	$ -	$ -	$ -	$ -	$ 2,000	$ -	$ -	$ -	$ -	$ -	$ -	$ 2,000
Insurance		250	-	-	-	-	-	-	-	-	-	-	-	250
Rent		500	500	500	500	500	500	500	500	500	500	500	500	6,000
Interest - Loan		-	-	-	-	-	-	-	-	-	-	-	-	-
Interest - Mortgage		-	-	-	-	-	-	-	-	-	-	-	-	-
Salaries		6,000	6,000	6,000	6,000	6,000	6,000	6,000	6,000	6,000	6,000	6,000	6,000	72,000
Advertising		500	500	500	500	500	500	500	500	500	500	500	500	6,000
Dues & Subscriptions		100	-	-	-	-	-	-	-	-	-	-	-	100
Legal & Accounting		-	-	900	-	-	-	-	-	-	-	-	-	900
Office Supplies		25	25	25	25	25	25	25	25	25	25	25	25	300
Telephone		50	50	50	50	50	50	50	50	50	50	50	50	600
Utilities		100	100	100	100	100	100	100	100	100	100	100	100	1,200
Website Fees		250	250	250	250	250	250	250	250	250	250	250	250	3,000
Total Expenses		$ 7,775	$ 7,425	$ 8,325	$ 7,425	$ 7,425	$ 7,425	$ 7,425	$ 7,425	$ 7,425	$ 7,425	$ 7,425	$ 7,425	$ 90,350
Ending Cash		$ 13,415	$ 16,790	$ 16,115	$ 16,640	$ 17,165	$ 17,690	$ 18,365	$ 19,040	$ 19,715	$ 20,390	$ 36,465	$ 52,540	

Year 3 Cash Flow Projections for THE ONLINE GAME BOY STORE

	Price	January	February	March	April	May	June	July	August	Sept	Oct	Nov	Dec	Totals
Beginning Cash		$ 52,540	$ 60,365	$ 68,540	$ 71,415	$ 75,190	$ 78,965	$ 82,740	$ 86,515	$ 89,890	$ 93,265	$ 96,640	$ 124,015	
Number of Customers per Month														
Revenues														
New Hardware Sales	$ 85	$ 8,500	$ 8,500	$ 6,800	$ 6,800	$ 6,800	$ 6,800	$ 6,800	$ 5,950	$ 5,950	$ 5,950	$ 42,500	$ 42,500	
Used Hardware Sales	$ 60	$ 18,000	$ 18,000	$ 9,000	$ 9,000	$ 9,000	$ 9,000	$ 9,000	$ 9,000	$ 9,000	$ 9,000	$ 12,000	$ 12,000	
New Game Sales	$ 30	$ 18,000	$ 18,000	$ 15,000	$ 15,000	$ 15,000	$ 15,000	$ 15,000	$ 15,000	$ 15,000	$ 15,000	$ 24,000	$ 24,000	
Used Game Sales	$ 10	$ 6,000	$ 6,000	$ 5,000	$ 5,000	$ 5,000	$ 5,000	$ 5,000	$ 5,000	$ 5,000	$ 5,000	$ 8,000	$ 8,000	
Total Revenues		$ 50,500	$ 50,500	$ 35,800	$ 35,800	$ 35,800	$ 35,800	$ 35,800	$ 34,950	$ 34,950	$ 34,950	$ 86,500	$ 86,500	$ 557,850
Total COGS		$ 30,900	$ 30,900	$ 20,600	$ 20,600	$ 20,600	$ 20,600	$ 20,600	$ 20,150	$ 20,150	$ 20,150	$ 47,700	$ 47,700	$ 320,650
Expenses														
Purchases		$ -	$ -	$ -	$ -	$ -	$ 2,000	$ -	$ -	$ -	$ -	$ -	$ -	$ 2,000
Insurance		$ 250	$ -	$ -	$ -	$ -	$ -	$ -	$ -	$ -	$ -	$ -	$ -	$ 250
Rent		$ 500	$ 500	$ 500	$ 500	$ 500	$ 500	$ 500	$ 500	$ 500	$ 500	$ 500	$ 500	$ 6,000
Interest - Loan		$ -	$ -	$ -	$ -	$ -	$ -	$ -	$ -	$ -	$ -	$ -	$ -	$ -
Interest - Mortgage		$ -	$ -	$ -	$ -	$ -	$ -	$ -	$ -	$ -	$ -	$ -	$ -	$ -
Salaries		$ 10,000	$ 10,000	$ 10,000	$ 10,000	$ 10,000	$ 10,000	$ 10,000	$ 10,000	$ 10,000	$ 10,000	$ 10,000	$ 10,000	$ 120,000
Advertising		$ 500	$ 500	$ 500	$ 500	$ 500	$ 500	$ 500	$ 500	$ 500	$ 500	$ 500	$ 500	$ 6,000
Dues & Subscriptions		$ 100	$ -	$ -	$ -	$ -	$ -	$ -	$ -	$ -	$ -	$ -	$ -	$ 100
Legal & Accounting		$ -	$ -	$ 900	$ -	$ -	$ -	$ -	$ -	$ -	$ -	$ -	$ -	$ 900
Office Supplies		$ 25	$ 25	$ 25	$ 25	$ 25	$ 25	$ 25	$ 25	$ 25	$ 25	$ 25	$ 25	$ 300
Telephone		$ 50	$ 50	$ 50	$ 50	$ 50	$ 50	$ 50	$ 50	$ 50	$ 50	$ 50	$ 50	$ 600
Utilities		$ 100	$ 100	$ 100	$ 100	$ 100	$ 100	$ 100	$ 100	$ 100	$ 100	$ 100	$ 100	$ 1,200
Website Fees		$ 250	$ 250	$ 250	$ 250	$ 250	$ 250	$ 250	$ 250	$ 250	$ 250	$ 250	$ 250	$ 3,000
Total Expenses		$ 11,775	$ 11,425	$ 12,325	$ 11,425	$ 11,425	$ 11,425	$ 11,425	$ 11,425	$ 11,425	$ 11,425	$ 11,425	$ 11,425	$ 138,350
Ending Cash		$ 60,365	$ 68,540	$ 71,415	$ 75,190	$ 78,965	$ 82,740	$ 86,515	$ 89,890	$ 93,265	$ 96,640	$ 124,015	$ 151,390	

APPENDIX A

BIOGRAPHIES OF THE PRINCIPALS

George and Mary have been married for 18 years and have three children, Adam, age 16 and Emily, age 14, and Ian, age 9. Mary Johnson has a degree from the University of North Carolina where she majored in elementary education. She taught for three years with the Brooklyn New York Department of Education. Upon moving to Anywhere, she has been teaching at the John Hay Elementary School in Anywhere. George is 42 years old and Mary is 40. They have lived in Anywhere for the past 15 years and participate in a number of community, school and church activities.

George Johnson received his degree in Textile Engineering and after spending three years as a Reserve Naval Officer took a position with the Yorkville Yarn Company in Anywhere. He has been with the company 15 years. His last position was Assistant Chief Engineer. George has also taken many classes on web development and Internet marketing.

George has had considerable retail store experience since he worked at his father's hardware store while in high school and during his summer vacations while attending the University of Minnesota. During his term of service in the Navy, he was stationed at the Brooklyn Naval Shipyard and became very acquainted with store operations.

This acquaintance gradually grew into a favorite pastime in that both expressed a desire to some day have their own business. The Internet has always been a fascination to them.

Due to the fact that the Yorkville Yarn Company has been sold, and the company will be moved from Anywhere, George has been given the option of moving or losing his position. He and Mary decided it would be in their best interest to start their own business. Accordingly, with their

love of technology and kid's video game, they now wish to open their own Internet business. Mary has given notice that she will only be available for substitute teaching since both will devote full time to operating and running THE ONLINE GAME BOY STORE.